10

2007 USA
39¢ Ella Fitzgerald,
Black Heritage #4120

11

2010 Canada
63¢ Queen Elisabeth II
#2617i

12

2000 USA
33¢ Figure Skating
#3190e

13

2016 Canada
Queen Elizabeth II
#2888

14

2003 USA
37¢ Child in a Straw Hat
by Mary Cassatt #3807

15

1923 USA
4¢ Martha Washington
#840

16

1904 USA
29c Ethel Merman,
Popular Singer #2853

17

1975 USA
10¢ Sybil Ludington,
Youthful Heroine #1559

18

2000 Canada
46¢ P. Vanier & E. Smellie,
Humanitarian #1825b

19

2000 Canada
46¢ Women are Persons
1823b

20

2018 Canada Nancy
Greene, Women in
Winter Sports #3079a

21

2008 USA
41¢ Marjorie K. Rawlings,
Writer #4223

22

2018 Canada
Danielle Goyette Women
in Winter Sports #3079c

23

1974 USA
18¢ Elizabeth Blackwell, 1st
Woman Physician #1399

24

2003 USA 37¢ Zora
Hurston, Singer #3748

31

2014 USA 49¢ Shirley
Chisholm, #4856

25

2002 Canada
48¢ Women's Hockey
Olympic Games #1939

26

1992 USA 32¢
Bessie Coleman, Black
Heritage #2956

27

2000 USA 33¢
Patricia R. Harris, Black
Heritage #3371

28

1998 USA
32¢ Madam C. J. Walker,
Black Heritage #3181

29

1990 USA
25¢ Helene Madison,
Olympian #2500

30

2018 USA
50¢ Lena Horne,
Black Heritage #5259

I0837683

Women on U.S. & Canadian Stamps

FEBRUARY

SUNDAY	MONDAY	TUESDAY	WEDNESDAY	THURSDAY	FRIDAY	SATURDAY

1

2001 USA
34¢ Scooties by Rose
O'Neill #3151

2

2009 Canada
54¢ Rosemary Brown
Black History #2315

3

2014 Canada
63¢ Barbara Ann Scott,
Winter Sports #2705

4

1986 USA
22¢ Sojourner Truth,
Black Heritage #2203

5

1940 USA
5¢ Louisa May Alcott,
Author #862

6

2011 Canada
59¢ Carrie Best Black
History Month #2433

7

2014 Canada
63¢ Sarah Burke, Winter
Sports #2707

8

2017 USA
49¢ Dorothy Height,
Black Heritage #5171

9

1998 USA
32¢ Gibson Girl, Fashion
in the 1900s 3282m

10

2013 USA
46¢ Rosa Parks
#4742

11

2013 USA
46¢ Rosa Parks
#4742

12

1987 USA
14¢ Julia Ward Howe
#2176

13

2014 Canada
63¢ Sandra Schmirler,
Winter Sports 2704b

2021 CALENDAR
WOMEN
ON U.S. AND CANADIAN
STAMPS

2013 USA Lydia Mendoza,
Music Icon #4786

1994 USA 29¢ Billie
Holiday, Jazz Singer #2856

1979 Canada Emile
Nelligan, Le Vaisseau

1996 USA 50¢ Jacque-
line Cochran, Pioneer

1998 USA 32¢ 19th
Amendment #3184e

2016 Canada Women's
Suffrage - 100 Anniversary

1998 USA 32¢ Flappers
Do the Charleston

1999 USA 33¢ Women's
Rights Movement #3189j

1997 USA 32¢ Lily Pons,
Opera Singer #3154

HAMEL PUBLICATIONS
BY PAUL J. HAMEL

Women on U.S. & Canadian Stamps

JANUARY

SUNDAY	MONDAY	TUESDAY	WEDNESDAY	THURSDAY	FRIDAY	SATURDAY
					1	**2**

1893 U.S. $1 Queen Isabella Pledging her Jewels #241 | 1952 USA
3¢ Betsy Ross #1004 |
| **3** | **4** | **5** | **6** | **7** | **8** | **9** |
| 

1872 Canada
6¢ Queen Victoria #39 | 

1978 USA
13¢ Harriet Tubman, Black Heritage #1744 | 1909 USA
8¢ Martha Washington #306 | 

2006 USA
39¢ Hattie McDaniel, Black Heritage - #3996 | 

1976 Canada 20¢+5¢ Women's Basketball Olympic Games #B12 | 

2009 USA
42¢ Mary Terrell & Mary White Ovington #4384a | 

2009 USA
42¢ Oswald Villard & Daisy Bates #4384c |

14

*2018 Canada
Kathleen Livingstone,
Black History #3085*

15

*1872 Canada
2¢ Queen Victoria
#36*

16

*2001 USA
34¢ Jessie Willcox
Smith #3502i*

17

*2000 Canada
46¢ Hilda Marion Neatby,
Historian #1829d*

18
*1999 USA
33¢ Women Support
War Effort #1386e*

19
*2001 USA
34¢ Neysa McMein,
Illustrators 3502m*

20
*2017 Canada
Adrianne Pieczonka,
Opera #2973*

21

*1989 #2403
25¢ North Dakota
Statehood*

22

*2010 Canada
57¢ Cross-country
Sprint Olympics #2374*

23
*2020 USA
(55¢) Gwen Ifill, Black
Heritage #5423*

24
*1984 USA
40¢ Lillian M. Gilbreth
#1868*

25
*2003 USA
37¢ Edith Head
#3772c*

26

*2009 USA
42¢ Medgar Evers &
Fannie L. Hamer #4384e*

27
*2009 USA
42¢ Ella Baker & Ruby
Hurley #4384f*

28

*1987 USA
2¢ Mary Lyon #2169*

Women on U.S. & Canadian Stamps

M A R C H

SUNDAY	MONDAY	TUESDAY	WEDNESDAY	THURSDAY	FRIDAY	SATURDAY
	1	**2**	**3**	**4**	**5**	**6**

	1977 Canada 12¢ Queen Elizabeth II #714	1999 USA 33¢ Alfred Lunt & Lynn Fontanne #3287	1997 USA 29¢ My Fair Lady, Stage and Screen, #2770	1981 Canada 17¢ Idola Saint-Jean Feminists #881	1985 USA 22¢ Mary M. Bethune, Black Heritage #2137	2008 USA 41¢ Gerty Cori, Biochemist #4224
7	**8**	**9**	**10**	**11**	**12**	**13**

2013 USA 32¢ Georgia O'Keeffe, Modern Artist, #3069	2016 Canada Women's Suffrage - 100th Anniversary #2901	1996 USA 50¢ Jacqueline Cochran, Pioneer Pilot #3066	1961 Canada 5¢ E. Pauline Johnson, Poet #518	1993 Canada 43¢ Helen Alice Kinnear, Legal Pioneer #1495	1987 USA 22¢ Girl Scouts of America #2251	1981 Canada 17¢ Emily Stowe, Feminists #879a

14	15	16	17	18	19	20
1993 Canada 43¢ Marie-Josephine Gerin-Lajoie #1459a	1991 Canada Jennie K. Trout, Physician #1305a	2011 USA (44¢) Carmen Miranda, Music Legends #4498	1993 Canada 43¢ Adelaide S. Hoodless, Educator 1495a	1972 USA 8¢ Family Planning #1455	2001 Canada Figure Skating Championships #1899	1852 USA 75¢ Harriet Beecher Stowe, Author #3430

21	22	23	24	25	26	27
1993 Canada 43¢ Pitseolak, Inuit Artist #1459a	1994 Canada 43¢ Jeanne Sauve, 1st Woman Governor General #1509	1990 USA 25¢ Judy Garland in Wizard of Oz #2245	1993 USA 29¢ Grace Kelly, Actor #2749	1975 USA 18¢ Elizabeth Blackwell, 1st Woman Physician #1399	1985 Canada 32¢ Therese Casgrain, Feminist #1047	2019 Canada Elsie MacGill Canadians in Flight #3172

28	29	30	31
1940 USA 5¢ Frances E. Willard, Educator #872	2016 USA (49¢) Sarah Vaughan Music Icons #5059	1981 Canada 17¢ Louise McKinney, Feminist #882a	1936 USA 3¢ Susan B. Anthony #784

Mar 1 First Day of Women's History Month

Mar 17 St. Patrick's Day

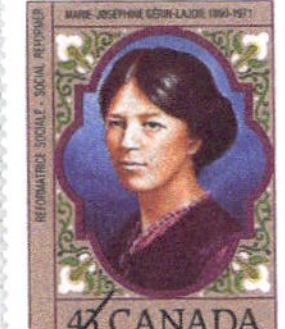

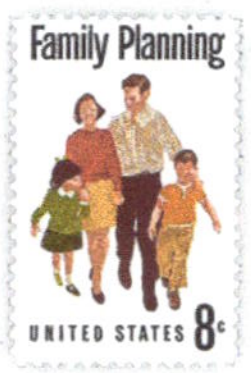

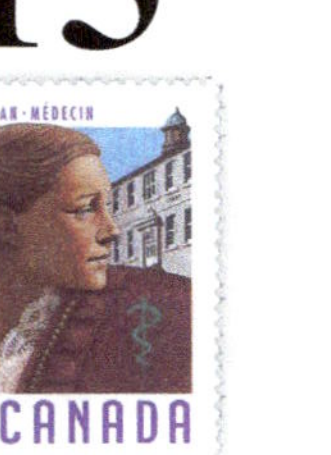

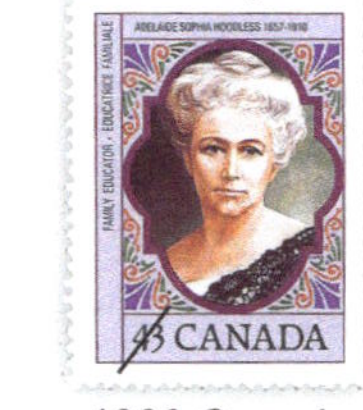

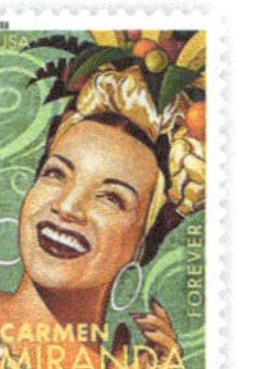

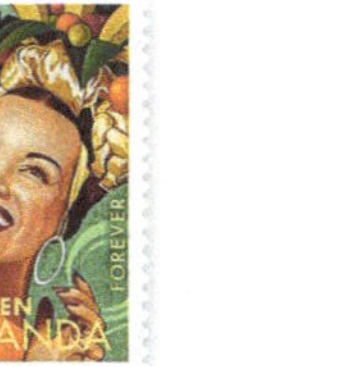

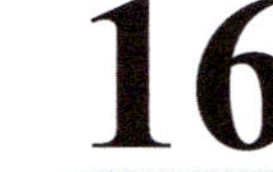

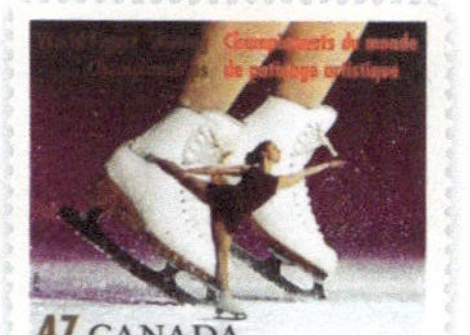

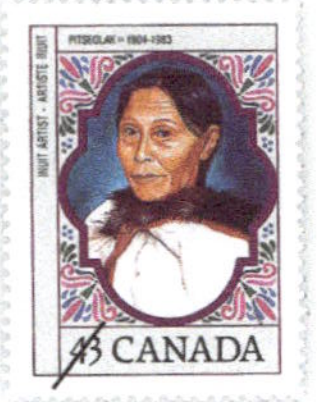

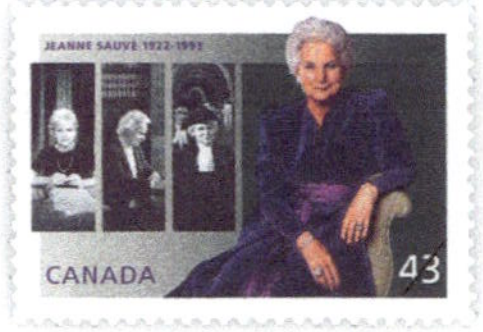

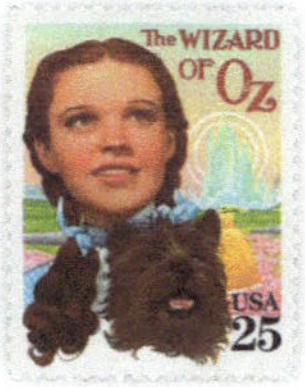

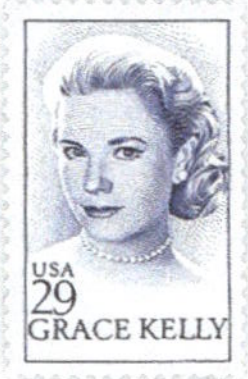

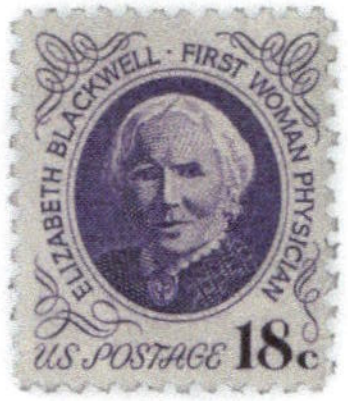

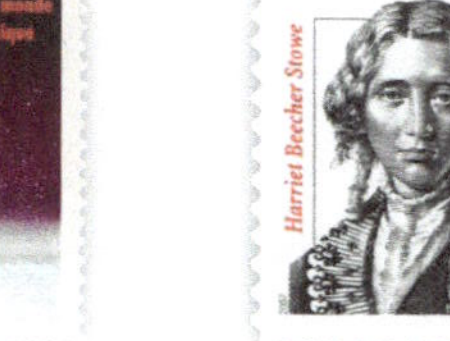

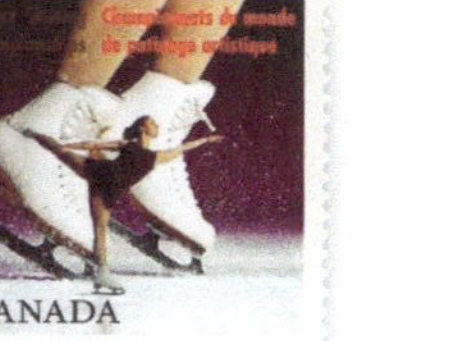

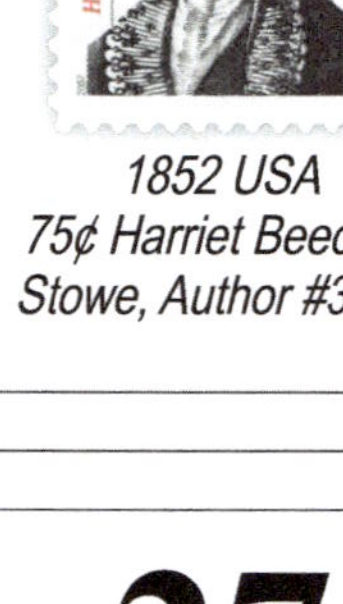

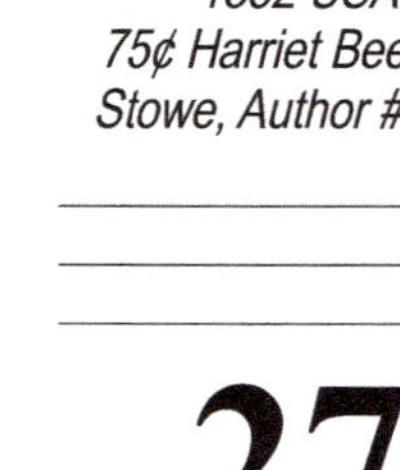

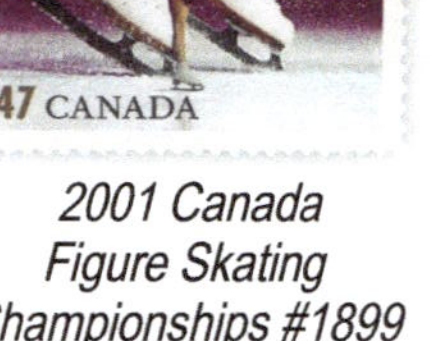

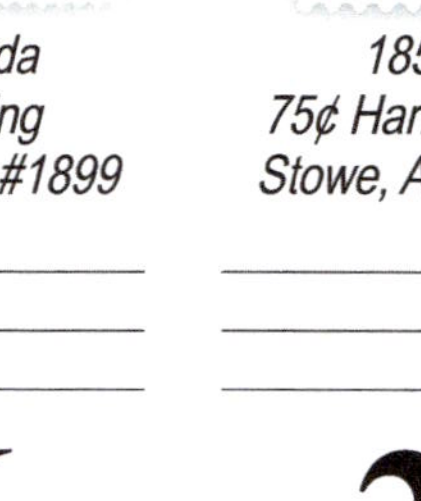

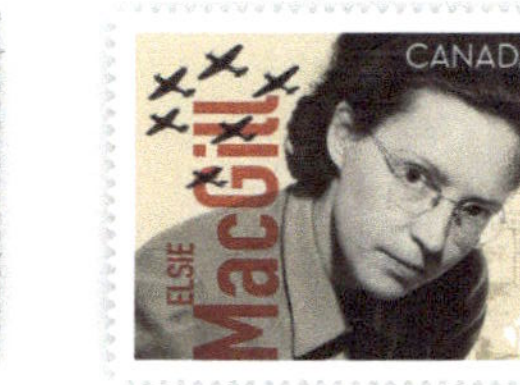

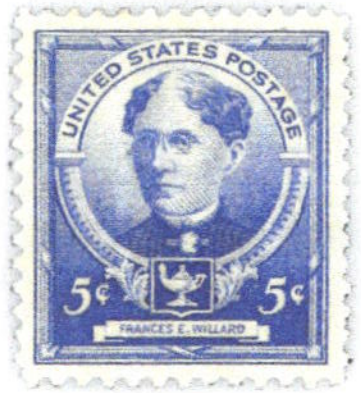

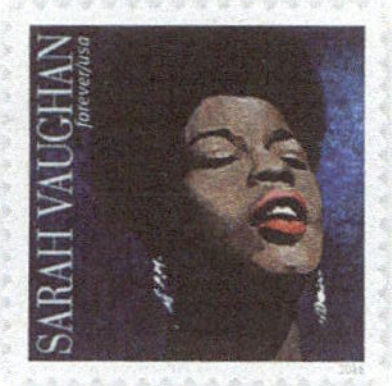

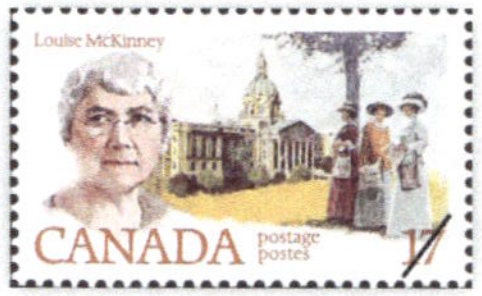

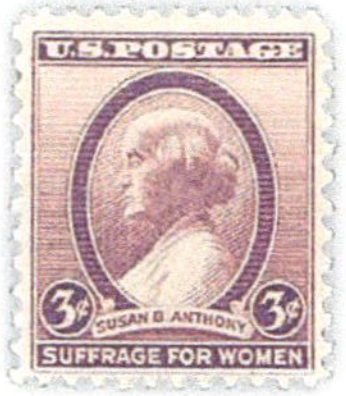

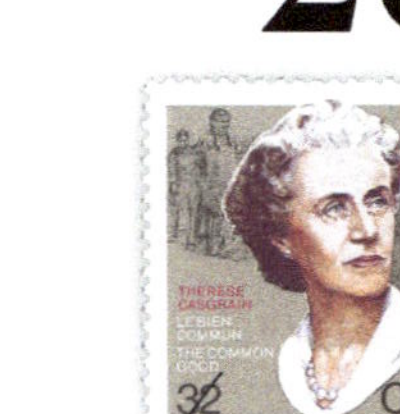

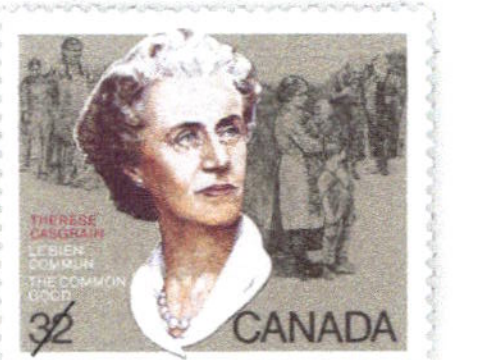

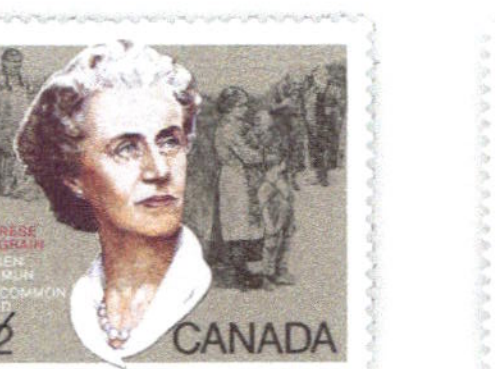

Women on U.S. & Canadian Stamps

APRIL

SUNDAY	MONDAY	TUESDAY	WEDNESDAY	THURSDAY	FRIDAY	SATURDAY

Apr 4 Easter Sunday
Apr 5 Easter Monday
Apr 15 Tax Day

1

2012 USA
(45¢) Gwendolyn Brooks,
Poet #4655

2

2012 USA
(45¢) Sylvia Plath,
Literature #4658

3

2003 USA
37¢ Liberty Carving of
Woman and Flag #3780

4

2012 USA
(45¢) Denise Levertov,
Literature #4661

5

2008 USA
42¢ Martha Gellhorn,
Literature #4248

6

2000 USA
33¢ Louise Nevelson,
Art & Photography #3383

7

2015 USA
(49¢) Maya Angelou,
Literature #4979

8

2015 Canada
"La Voie Lactee" by Gen-
evieve Cadieux, #2822

9

2005 USA
37¢ Marian Anderson,
Music #3896

10

2005 USA
15¢ Frances Perkins,
Singer #1821

11

2017 Canada
Vimy Ridge design by
Susan Scott, #2982

12

2016 Canada
Toronto by Lutz Dille,
Photography #2902

13

2016 Canada
"Window" by Angela
Grauerholz #2903

14

1986 Canada
34¢ Koñwatsi'tsiaieñni,
Iroquois leader #1091

15

2011 USA
84¢ Olveta Culp Hobby,
Stateswoman #4510

16

1971 USA
(44¢) Selena,
Musician #4499

17

1985 Canada
32¢ Emily Murphy,
Feminist #1048

18

1990 USA
25¢ Marianne Moore,
Poet #2449

19

2016 USA
(47¢) Shirley Temple,
Hollywood Legend #5060

20

2018 Canada
Queen Elizabeth II - 65th
Anniversary #3098

21

2012 USA
(45¢) Elizabeth Bishop,
Poet #4659

22

1999 USA
33¢ Ayn Rand, Literary
Arts #3308

23

2019 USA
(55¢) Maureen Connolly
Brinker, Tennis #5377

24

1981 Canada
17¢ Kateri Tekakwitha,
Religious Personality #885

25

2011 USA
(44¢) Helen Hayes,
Stage and Screen #4525

26

1907 USA
5¢ Pocahontas, Native
American Heritage #330

27

1994 USA
29¢ Theda Bara, Stage
& Screen #2827

28

1994 USA
29¢ Clara Bow, Stage
& Screen #2820

29

2020 Canada
Veronica Foster , Ronnie
the Bren Gun Girl #2020

30

1994 USA
29¢ Zasu Pitts, Stage
& Screen #2824

Women on U.S. & Canadian Stamps

M A Y

SUNDAY	MONDAY	TUESDAY	WEDNESDAY	THURSDAY	FRIDAY	SATURDAY

May 5 Cinco de Mayo
May 9 Mother's Day
May 31 Memorial Day

1

1969 USA
6¢ Grandma Moses,
Artist #1370

2

1996 USA
32¢ Women's Diving,
Olympics #3068b

3

1979 Canada
Emile Nelligan, Le Vais-
seau d'or, Author #818a

4

2004 USA
37¢ Martha Graham,
Choreographer # 3840

5

1938 USA
1½¢ Martha
Washington #805

6

1970 #1390
6¢ Age of Reptiles

7

2015 Canada
FIFA Women's World
Cup #2837a

8

2013 Canada
Queen Elizabeth II 60th
Anniversary #2644i

15

1975 Canada 8¢ Lucy M. Montgomery, Anne of Green Gables #658

14
1996 USA 32¢ Women's Gymnastics #3068g

13
1959 Canada Associated Country Women of the World #385

12
2010 USA 44¢ Katharine Hepburn, Actor #4461

11
1975 USA 50¢ Harriet Quimby, Pioneer Pilot #C128

10
1996 USA 32¢ Women's Running, Olympics #3068c

9

1934 USA 3¢ Mothers of America by Whistler #737

22
2012 Canada Louise Arbour, Humanitarian #2550i

21
2008 Canada 96¢ Audrey Hepburn by Yousuf Karsh #2172a

20
1980 USA 15¢ Dolley Madison, First Lady #1822

19
2009 USA 78¢ Mary Lasker, Philanthropist #3432b

18
USA 37¢ Margaret La Farge Osborn by I. Noguchi #3858

17
2006 USA 39¢ Anne Porter, Literature #4030

16

2013 USA (46¢) Lydia Mendoza, Music Icon #4786

29

1998 USA 32¢ Flappers Do the Charleston #3184b

28
1998 USA 3 2¢ 19th Amendment #3184e

27
2010 USA 44¢ Kate Smith, Singer #4463

26
1999 USA 33¢ I Love Lucy, Stage & Screen #3187l

25
2006 USA 39¢ Amber Alert #4031

24
1967 5¢ Canada Votes for Women #470

31
1980 USA 15¢ Emily Bissell, #1823

23
1996 USA 32¢ Georgia O'Keeffe #3069

30

2006 USA 39¢ Frances Willis, Diplomat #4076b

Women on U.S. & Canadian Stamps

J U N E

SUNDAY	MONDAY	TUESDAY	WEDNESDAY	THURSDAY	FRIDAY	SATURDAY
		1  1995 USA 32¢ Marilyn Monroe, Hollywood Legend #2967	**2**  1960 USA 4¢ American Woman #1152	**3**  1994 Canada 43¢ Bond Between Generations #1523	**4** 2009 USA 44¢ Anna Julia Cooper, Black Heritage #3308	**5** 2015 USA (93¢) Flannery O'Connor, Literary Arts #5003
6 1974 USA 10¢ Lovely Reader by J.E. Liotard #1533	**7**  2002 USA 37¢ Gertrude Käsebier, Photographer #3649d	**8**  1982 USA 20¢ The Barrymores, Performing Arts #2012	**9**  2002 USA 37¢ Imogen Cunningham, Photographer #3649q	**10**  1981 USA 18¢ Edna St. Vincent Millay, Poet #1926	**11**    2003 USA 37¢ Audrey Hepburn, Hollywood Legend #3786	**12**  2012 USA (45¢) Edith Piaf, Singer #4692

19

1897 Canada
2¢ Queen Victoria Jubilee issue #52

18

1986 USA
17¢ Belva Ann Lockwood, Educator #2178

17

2007 USA
58¢ Margaret Chase Smith, Senator #3427

16

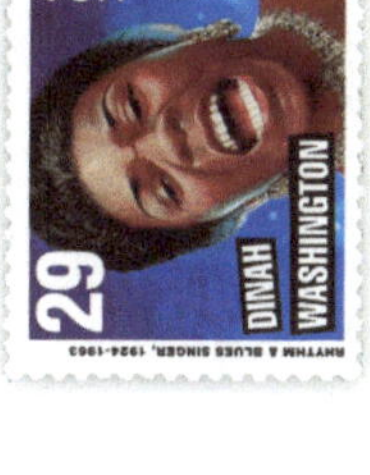

1993 USA
29¢ Dinah Washington, Music Legend #2730

15

1996 USA
32¢ Breast Cancer Awareness #1308

14

1985 USA
22¢ Abigail Adams, Political Figure #2146

13

2002 USA
37¢ Migrant Mother by Dorothea Lange, #3649

26

1995 USA
32¢ Mary Chesnut, Diarist #2975o

25

1983 USA
5¢ Pearl Buck, Author #1884

24

1994 USA
29¢ Statue of Liberty #1041

23

1995 USA
32¢ Phoebe Pember, Nurse #2975r

22

2001 USA
34¢ Frida Kahlo, Artist #3509

21

2005 Canada
50¢ Ellen Louks Fairclough #2112

20

2008 Canada
52¢ Anne of Green Gables #2277

30

1986 USA
1¢ Margaret Mitchell, Literature #2168

29

2007 Canada
52¢ Joni Mitchell, Recording Artists #2221b

28

1995 USA
32¢ Harriet Tubman, Abolitionist #2975k

27

1980 USA
15¢ Helen Keller & Anne Sullivan, Education #1824

Jun 19 Juneteenth
Jun 20 Father's Day

Women on U.S. & Canadian Stamps

JULY

SUNDAY	MONDAY	TUESDAY	WEDNESDAY	THURSDAY	FRIDAY	SATURDAY

1

2011 Canada
Ginette Reno, Recording Artists #2482b

2

2010 Canada
57¢ Prudence Heward - Rollande Artist #2395

3

1998 Canada
45¢ Royal Canadian Women Mounted Police #1737b

4

1977 USA
13¢ The Seamstress for Independence #1717

5

2013 Canada
Stella by Marie-Louise Gay, Literature #2652

6

1990 USA
25¢ Hazel Wightman, Olympian #2498

7

2014 Canada
Lynne Cohen's "Untitled," Photography #2761

8

1996 Canada
Ethel Catherwood, Sporting Hero #1608

9

2020 USA
(55¢) Nella Larsen, Author #5471

10

2015 Canada
Alice Munro, Writer #2850

11

1995 USA
55¢ Alice Hamilton, MD,
Social Reformer #2940

12

1991 USA 29¢ Women
Summer Olympics
Gymnastics # 2638

13

2000 USA
33¢ Stamp Design by
Morgan Hill, Artist #3416

14

2004 USA
23¢ Wilma Rudolph,
Athlete #3422

15

1998 USA
32¢ Mahalia Jackson,
Music Legend #3216

16 

1998 USA
32¢ Lila & DeWitt Wallace,
Philanthropists #2936

17

1998 USA
32¢ Roberta Martin,
Gospel Singer #3217

18

1998 USA
32¢ Rosetta Tharpe,
Gospel Singer #3219

19

1948 USA
3¢ Progress of Women
#959

20

2006 USA
Wonder Woman, Comic
Superhero #4084c

21

1991 USA
29¢ Women Sprinters,
Olympics #2555

22 

1909 USA
(45¢) Katherine Dunham,
Stage and Screen #4700

23

1998 USA
32¢ Clara Ward, Gospel
Singer #3218

24

1962 USA
4¢ Girl Scout #1199

25 

2008 Canada
52¢ Lifesaving
Society #2282

26

2007 USA
41¢ Spider-Woman,
Super Hero #4159g

27 

2007 USA
41¢ Spider-Woman,
Super Hero #4159g

28

2012 USA
(45¢) Isadora Duncan,
Choreographer #5698

29

2002 USA
83¢ Edna Ferber,
Author #3434

30

1963 USA
8¢ Amelia Earhart,
Pilot #C68

31

2011 USA
(44¢) Celia Cruz, Music
Legend #4501

Women on U.S. & Canadian Stamps

AUGUST

SUNDAY	MONDAY	TUESDAY	WEDNESDAY	THURSDAY	FRIDAY	SATURDAY
1	**2**	**3**	**4**	**5**	**6**	**7**

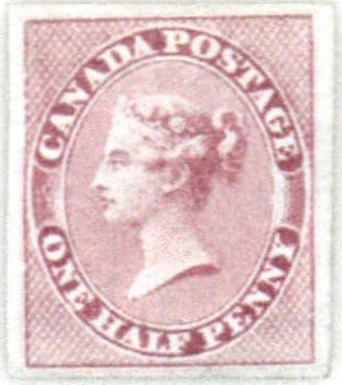

1857 Canada
½¢ Queen Victoria
#11

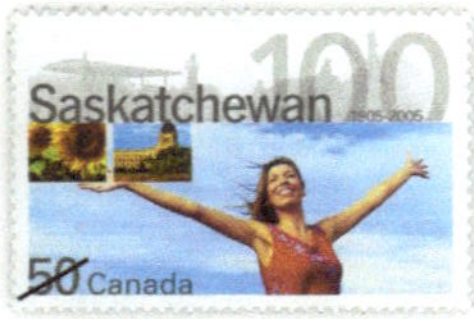

2005 Canada
50¢ Saskatchewan
#2117

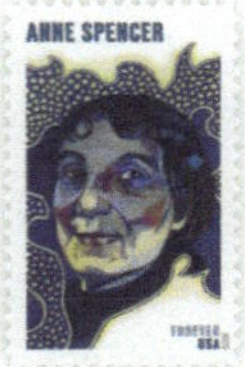

2020 USA
(55¢) Anne Spencer,
Poet #4573

2004 USA
37¢ Agnes de Mille,
Stage and Screen #3842

1994 Canada
43¢ High Jump,
Commonwealth Games #1502

2001 USA
34¢ Lucille Ball,
Hollywood Legend #3523

1988 USA
23¢ Mary Cassatt,
Artist #2181

8	**9**	**10**	**11**	**12**	**13**	**14**

2014 USA
(49¢) Janis Joplin, Music
Icon #4916

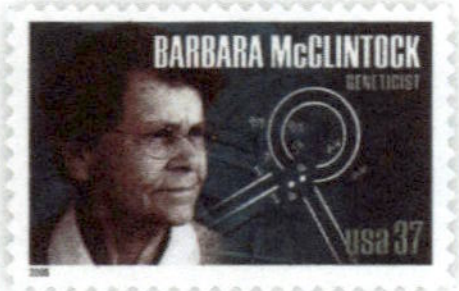

2005 USA
37¢ Barbara McClintock,
Geneticist #3906

2009 Canada
54¢ Ringette, Canadian
Inventions #2338b

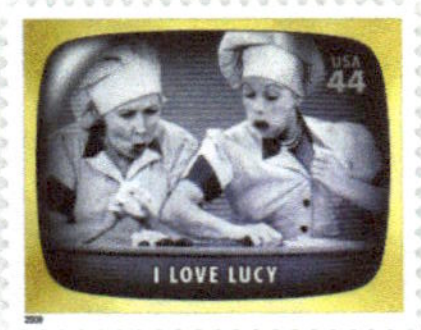

2009 USA
44¢ Lucille Ball & Vivian Vance
as Lucy & Ethel #4414b

1994 Canada
43¢ Mary Travers,
Chansonnière, #1526

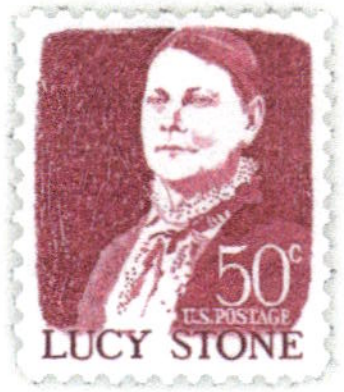

968 USA
50¢ Lucy Stone,
Humanitarian #1293

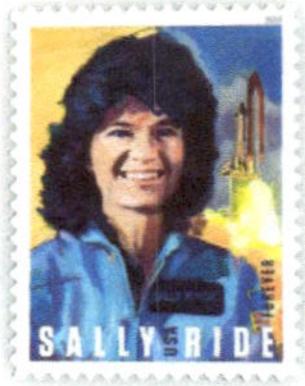

2018 USA
(50¢) Sally Ride, 1st
Woman in Space #5283

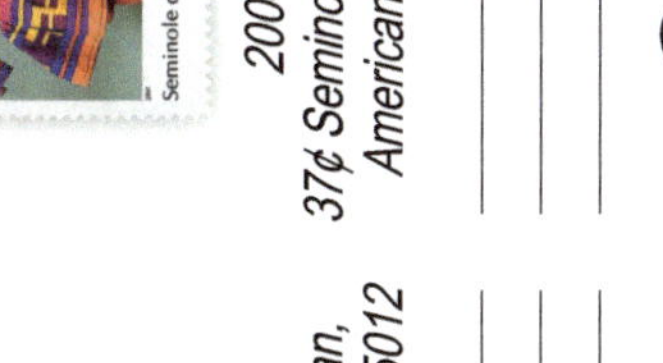

15

1998 Canada
Phyllis Munday, Legendary
Canadian #1751l

16

1979 Canada
Women's Field Hockey
Championship #834

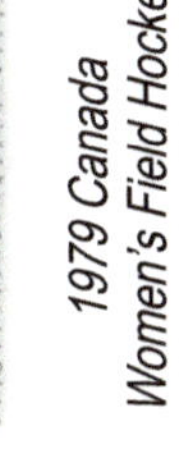

17

1992 USA
29¢ Women Join the
War Effort #2697h

18

1995 USA
78¢ Alice Paul,
Suffragist #2943

19

1981 USA
17¢ Rachel Carson,
Literature #1857

20

2015 USA
(49¢) Ingrid Bergman,
Hollywood Legend #5012

21

2004 USA
37¢ Seminole Doll, Native
American Art #3873e

22

1992 USA
29¢ Dorothy Parker,
Writer #2698

23

2013 USA
(46¢) Althea Gibson,
Tennis #4803

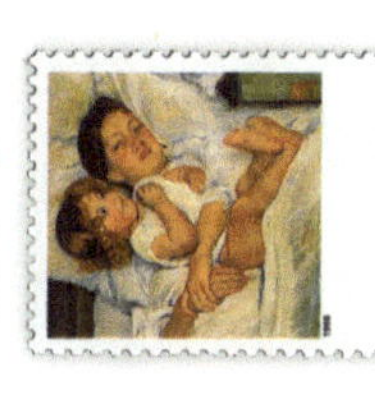

24

2006 USA
39¢ Gee's Bend
Quilts #4098

25

1955 USA
50¢ Susan B. Anthony,
Humanitarian #1051

26

1975 USA
10¢ International
Women's Year #1571

27

1998 USA
32¢ Breakfast in Bed by
Mary Cassatt, #3236O

28

1971 USA
8¢ Emily Dickinson,
Poet #1436

29

1991 USA
29¢ Fanny Brice,
Comedians #2565

30

1973 Canada
8¢ Nellie McClung,
#622

31

1976 USA 1
3¢ Clara Maass, Health
& Medicine #1699

Women on U.S. & Canadian Stamps

SEPTEMBER

SUNDAY	MONDAY	TUESDAY	WEDNESDAY	THURSDAY	FRIDAY	SATURDAY

1

1919 USA
3¢ Victory and Flags
of Allies #537

2

1995 USA
32¢ Refugees
#2981g

3

1997 Canada
45¢ Martha (Munger) Black,
Prominent Canadian #1661

4

2016 Canada
Elgin & Winter Garden,
Toronto Haunted #2935

5

1934 #745
6¢ Crater Lake

Sept 6 Labor Day

7

1948 USA
3¢ Clara Barton, Founder
of the Red Cross #967

8

2003 Canada
46¢ Susanna Moodie,
Author #1997a

9

1992 Canada
4¢ 2 Laura Secord, Patriot
Folklore Hero #1935

10

1997 USA
32¢ Lily Pons,
Opera Singer #3154

11

1952 USA
3¢ Service Women
#1013

1869 USA
10¢ Jane Addams,
Humanitarian #878

12

1966 USA
5¢ General Federation of
Women's Clubs #1316

13

1998 USA
32¢ Emily Post's
Etiquette #3184f

14

2018 Canada
Paramedics Emergency
Responders #3126

15

1976 Canada
10¢ Ceremonial Cos-
tume, Iroquoians #581a

16

2011 USA
(44¢) Barbara Jordan,
Black Heritage #4565

17

1994 USA
29¢ Mildred Bailey, Jazz
& Blues Singer # 2860

18

2008 USA
42¢ Bette Davis, Legend
of Hollywood #4350

19

2008 USA Woman
Olympic Gymnasts
#4334

20

1973 USA
8¢ Willa Cather,
Novelist #1487

21

1948 USA
3¢ Gold Star Mothers
#969

22

1981 USA
18¢ Babe Zaharias,
Golf #1932

23

1983 USA
1¢ Dorothea Dix,
Humanitarian #1844

24

1978 Canada
14¢ Woman Walking
Inuit, Travel #769

25

1993 USA
29¢ Carter Family, Country
& Western Music #2773

26

2014 USA
(49¢) Julia Child,
Celebrity Chef #4926

27

1972 USA
8¢ Mail Order
Business #1468

28

2005 USA
37¢ Miss Piggy of the
Muppets #3944d

29

1938 #833
$2 Warren G. Harding

30

1935 #774
3¢ Boulder Dam

Women on U.S. & Canadian Stamps

OCTOBER

SUNDAY	MONDAY	TUESDAY	WEDNESDAY	THURSDAY	FRIDAY	SATURDAY

1

2003 Canada
48¢ Julie Payette,
Astronaut #1999

2

1995 Canada
45¢ Nelvana, Comic
Book Superhero #1581

3

2014 USA
(49¢) Joyce Chen,
Celebrity Chef #4924

4

1971 USA
8¢ Prevent Drug
Abuse #1438

5

2014 USA
(49¢) Edna Lewis,
Celebrity Chef #4922

6

1993 USA
29¢ Patsy Cline, Country
Western Singer #2772

7

1994 USA
29¢ Billie Holiday,
Jazz Singer #2856

8

1998 USA
32¢ Holiday
Shopping #3111

9

1990 Canada
Agnes Macphail, Member
of Parliament #1293

10

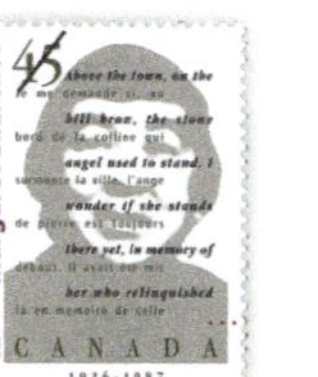

1996 Canada
45¢ Margaret Laurence,
Author #1626a

11

1963 USA
5¢ Eleanor Roosevelt
#1236

12

1974 USA
10¢ Disabled Children
#1549

13

1994 USA
29¢ 'Ma' Rainey,
Blues Singer #2859

14

2005 USA
37¢ Greta Garbo,
Stage & Screen #3943

15

1994 USA
29¢ Bessie Smith,
Jazz Singer #2854

16

1940 #899
1¢ Statue of Liberty

17

2006 Canada
51¢ Maureen Forrester,
Opera Singer #2178

18

1994 USA
29¢ Annie Oakley, Legend
of the West #2869d

19

1996 USA
32¢ Olympic Beach
Volleyball #3068k

20

1995 USA
46¢ Ruth Benedict,
Anthropologist #2938

21

1994 USA
29¢ Nellie Cashman,
Peace Maker #2869a

22

1994 USA
29¢ Sacagawea, Native
American Guide #2869s

23

1993 USA
29¢ Rebecca of Sunnybrook
Farm by Kate Wiggin #2785

24

1994 USA 20¢ Virginia
Apgar, Physician #2179

31

1984 USA 20¢ Hispanic-
Americans #2103

25

1983 USA
28¢ Women's Olympic
Gymnastics #C101

26

1964 USA
5¢ Homemakers
#1253

27

2013 Canada
63¢ Saint Anne with
the Christ Child 2688a

28

2006 Canada
51¢ Simoneau and
Alarie, Opera #2178

29

1948 USA
3¢ Juliette Gordon Low,
Girl Scot Founder #974

30

1993 USA
29¢ Little House on the Prairie
by Laura Wilder # 2786

Women on U.S. & Canadian Stamps

NOVEMBER

SUNDAY	MONDAY	TUESDAY	WEDNESDAY	THURSDAY	FRIDAY	SATURDAY
	1	**2**	**3**	**4**	**5**	**6**
	 1960 USA 4¢ Camp Fire Girls #1167	2005 Canada $1.45 Christmas Creche #2127	 2011 USA (44¢) Maria Goeppert Mayer, Physicist #4543	1966 USA 5¢ The Boating Party by Mary Cassatt # 1322	 1997 USA 32¢ Women in Military Service #3174	 1993 USA 29¢ Little Women by Louisa May Alcott #2788
7	**8**	**9**	**10**	**11**	**12**	**13**
1897 Canada 1¢ Queen Victoria #67	1041 Canada 40¢ Women's Armed Forces #1345	1948 USA 3¢ Moina Michael, Humanitarian #977	 2002 USA 37¢ Ida M. Tarbell, Literature #3666	2002 USA 37¢ Ethel L. Payne, Literature #3667	 2002 USA 37¢ Marguerite Higgins, Literature #3668	1992 Canada 48¢ La Befana, Christmas Personage #1453

14

2010 USA
44¢ Julia de Burgos,
Literary Artist #4477

15

1996 USA
32¢ Dorothy Fields,
Songwriter #3102

16

1980 USA
15¢ Edith Wharton,
Literature #1832

17

2006 USA
39¢ Wonder Woman
#4084m

18

1999 USA
33¢ Women's Rights
Movement #3189j

19

1997 USA
32¢ Rosa Ponselle,
Opera Singer #3157

20

1998 USA
32¢ Eleanor Roosevelt
and child #3185d

21

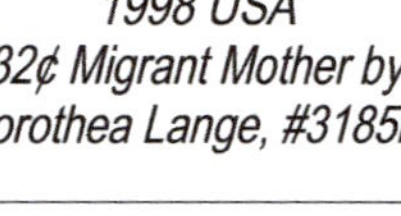

1998 USA
32¢ Migrant Mother by
Dorothea Lange, #3185m

22

1998 USA 32¢ Gone
With the Wind by
Margaret Mitchell #2446

23

1994 USA
29¢ Ethel Waters,
Popular Singer #2851

24

1995 USA
32¢ Woman Suffrage
#2980

25

1937 USA
5¢ Virginia Dare
#796

26

1982 USA
Dr. Mary Walker, Army
Surgeon #2013

27

1902 USA
8¢ Martha Washington
#306

28

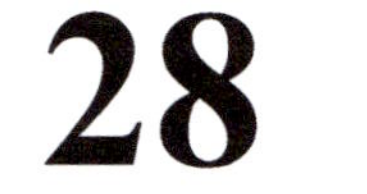

2009 USA
44¢ The Dinah Shore
Show #4414j

29

2009 USA
44¢ Burns and Allen
TV Show #4414p

30

2012 USA
(45¢) Lady Bird
Johnson #4716f

Nov 2 Election Day
Nov 11 Veterans Day
Nov 25 Thanksgiving Day
Nov 26 Black Friday

Women on U.S. & Canadian Stamps

DECEMBER

SUNDAY	MONDAY	TUESDAY	WEDNESDAY	THURSDAY	FRIDAY	SATURDAY

Dec 24 'Christmas Day' observed

Dec 24 Christmas Eve

Dec 25 Christmas Day

Dec 31 'New Year's Day' observed

Dec 31 New Year's Eve

1

1995 USA
32¢ Women's Suffrage
#1406

2

2009 USA
44¢ Kukla, Fran & Ollie,
(Fran Allison) TV # 4414k

3

2009 USA
44¢ Ozzie & Harriet
(Nelson) TV Show #4414q

4

1996 USA
35¢ Women Olympic
Swimming #3068n

5

2003 USA
37¢ Mary Cassatt -
On a Balcony #3806

6

1998 USA
32¢ Margret Mead,
Anthropologist, 3236b

7

1996 USA
32¢ Women's
Sailboarding # 3068h

8

1996 USA
32¢ Women's Olympic
Soccer #C111

9

1996 USA
32¢ Women's Olympic
Running #3068c

10

1996 USA
32¢ Women's Olympic
Swimming #3068d

11

2001 USA
(44¢) Greta von Nessen,
Designer #4546i

12

2014 Canada
Ghost Bride, Haunted
Canada #2749

13

2008 Canada
52¢ Marie Dressler Canadian
in Hollywood #2279

14

2005 Canada
85¢ Christmas Creche
#2126

15

1931 USA
2¢ The Greatest Mother,
Red Cross #702

16

1987 USA
22¢ Love you, Mother!
#2273

17

1999 Canada
46¢ Portia White,
Singer #1820a

18

2008 USA
42¢ Josephine Baker,
Prinsesse Tam-Tam #4338

19

2013 Canada
Laura Secord The War
of 1812 #1435

20

1980 Canada
17¢ Sedna, Inuit Spirit
#867a

21

2011 Canada
$1.75 Spiritual Renewal,
Daphne Odjig, Artist #2439

22

2003 Canada
48¢ Roberta Bondar,
Astronaut #1999

23

1984 USA
20¢ Eleanor
Roosevelt #2105

24

1998 USA 77¢ Mary
Breckenridge, Frontier
Nursing Service #2942

25

1989 USA
25¢ Madonna
and Child #2427

26

1981 USA
18¢ The Gift of Self,
Red Cross #1910

27

1983 USA
35¢ Women Fencing
#C109

28

1961 USA
4¢ Nursing
#1190

29

1998 USA
32¢ Boy Scouts & Girl
Scouts #3183j

30

1980 USA
28¢ Blanche Stuart
Scott, Pioneer Pilot #C99

31

1958 USA
3¢ Gardening –
Horticulture #1100

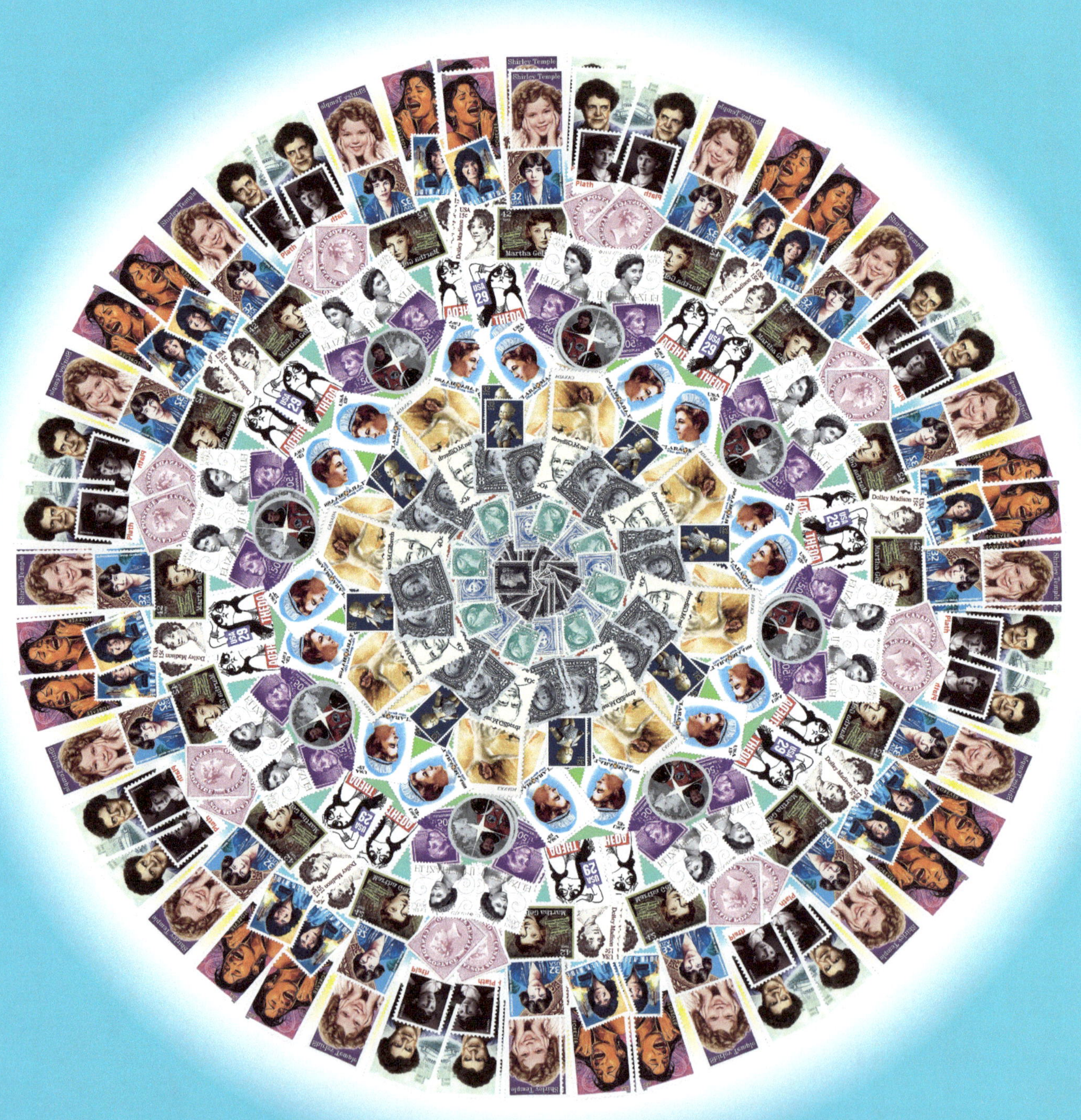

2021

January

S	M	T	W	T	F	S
					1	2
3	4	5	6	7	8	9
10	11	12	13	14	15	16
17	18	19	20	21	22	23
24	25	26	27	28	29	30
31						

February

S	M	T	W	T	F	S
	1	2	3	4	5	6
7	8	9	10	11	12	13
14	15	16	17	18	19	20
21	22	23	24	25	26	27
28						

March

S	M	T	W	T	F	S
	1	2	3	4	5	6
7	8	9	10	11	12	13
14	15	16	17	18	19	20
21	22	23	24	25	26	27
28	29	30	31			

April

S	M	T	W	T	F	S
				1	2	3
4	5	6	7	8	9	10
11	12	13	14	15	16	17
18	19	20	21	22	23	24
25	26	27	28	29	30	

May

S	M	T	W	T	F	S
						1
2	3	4	5	6	7	8
9	10	11	12	13	14	15
16	17	18	19	20	21	22
23	24	25	26	27	28	29
30	31					

June

S	M	T	W	T	F	S
		1	2	3	4	5
6	7	8	9	10	11	12
13	14	15	16	17	18	19
20	21	22	23	24	25	26
27	28	29	30			

July

S	M	T	W	T	F	S
				1	2	3
4	5	6	7	8	9	10
11	12	13	14	15	16	17
18	19	20	21	22	23	24
25	26	27	28	29	30	31

August

S	M	T	W	T	F	S
1	2	3	4	5	6	7
8	9	10	11	12	13	14
15	16	17	18	19	20	21
22	23	24	25	26	27	28
29	30	31				

September

S	M	T	W	T	F	S
			1	2	3	4
5	6	7	8	9	10	11
12	13	14	15	16	17	18
19	20	21	22	23	24	25
26	27	28	29	30		

October

S	M	T	W	T	F	S
					1	2
3	4	5	6	7	8	9
10	11	12	13	14	15	16
17	18	19	20	21	22	23
24	25	26	27	28	29	30
31						

November

S	M	T	W	T	F	S
	1	2	3	4	5	6
7	8	9	10	11	12	13
14	15	16	17	18	19	20
21	22	23	24	25	26	27
28	29	30				

December

S	M	T	W	T	F	S
			1	2	3	4
5	6	7	8	9	10	11
12	13	14	15	16	17	18
19	20	21	22	23	24	25
26	27	28	29	30	31	